THE ART OF SPIRITUAL WARFARE

ALSO FROM REVIVAL TODAY

Financial Overflow

Dominion Over Sickness and Disease

Boldly I Come

Twenty Secrets for an Unbreakable Marriage

How to Dominate in a Wicked Nation

Seven Wrong Relationships

Everything a Man Should Be

Understanding the World in Light of Bible Prophecy

Are You Going Through a Crisis?

The 20 Laws that Govern the Financial Anointing

35 Questions for Those Who Hate the Prosperity Gospel

The Art of Spiritual Warfare

Books are available in EBOOK and PAPERBACK through your favorite online book retailer or by request from your local bookstore.

THE ART OF SPIRITUAL WARFARE

JONATHAN SHUTTLESWORTH

RISE UP
PUBLICATIONS

Rise UP Publications
644 Shrewsbury Commons Ave
Ste 249
Shrewsbury PA 17361
United States of America
www.riseUPpublications.com
Phone: 866-846-5123

CONTENTS

INTRODUCTION

"Rise, take your journey, and cross over the river Arnon.
Look, I have given into your hand Sihon the Amorite, king
of Heshbon, and his land. Begin to possess it, and engage
him in battle."

— DEUTERONOMY 2:24 (NKJV)

That poor king was living in a land he thought was his. He had the proper paperwork but didn't realize God had already transferred the land to Moses. But Moses couldn't walk right in and take it. He had to engage him in battle and begin to possess it.

The things God's given to you don't drop into your lap. You must fight for what God says is yours. Health and healing belong to you, but you must fight for them because forces oppose your inheritance.

Nobody scoots up the sideline into the end zone without an opponent trying to tackle them. There are forces in opposition to you going to Heaven. Forces are resisting your healing and your continued health. Forces are resisting your prosperity. Some people have parents who worked their whole lives and retired with nothing, and now, they depend on their children to supplement their income each month.

You don't stumble into prosperity, healing, Heaven, or victory over sin—it's a fight. If life is a fight, it's good to know how to win the fight! Can you win the fight?

Fighting is inevitable. In my late teens and twenties, I thought by doing everything right when I went into ministry, I wouldn't have any troubles. Back in the '80s, I saw TV exposés and critiques of some TV ministers. I thought, 'Well I'm not going to do what those guys did. I won't be a flamboyant minister. I won't do showy stuff that attracts attention. I'll just be a nice, normal minister. Then, I won't have any problems.' I must have missed the part in the Bible about the character named Jesus. Jesus did everything right. He treated people right, never sinned, and had the highest ethical standards. He was kind and compassionate. Newspapers didn't run an exposé on Him; He didn't make headlines. What they did was put Him to death, even though He did nothing wrong in His entire life.

You learn from attacks against you, your destiny, your dreams, and your advancement. Your wrongdoing does not cause the attacks, they come because God's anointing on your life attracts adversaries.

When Joseph announced his dream, his family turned on him. His brothers sought to kill him. When God marks you for a glorious destiny, it's a magnet for confrontation. But you can prevail in those confrontations 100 percent of the time. This book will deal with that through 24 practical, actionable keys.

If you're anointed, you are guaranteed to face battles. Just make sure you're anointed and not acting like an idiot. If you have a big destiny, you'll have a lot of enemies. But having a lot of enemies doesn't mean you have a big destiny. It can also mean you're stupid about how you treat people and you make bad decisions.

If I decide to stop paying my taxes for the next five years, I'll probably end up in a huge battle with the IRS and face going to federal prison. If that happened, it wouldn't be because I have a great destiny. It's simply because I didn't pay my taxes. I acted foolishly and faced the consequences. Don't conflate those two things. We are not a ministry that celebrates turmoil. Life doesn't have to be filled with chaos. Even when storms raise their head, God will give you peace.

When I talk about spiritual warfare, I'm talking about real battles. I'm not talking about waving colored flags or blowing shofars. I'm talking about actual battles like the one in Deuteronomy 2:24 when God gave them land to possess, but the people occupying it didn't want to give it up. Yet God said, "Engage him in battle and begin to possess it."

I'm discussing spiritual warfare that produces land ownership, buildings, property, and financial fortune. I'm talking about fighting for children who are not serving the Lord to start serving the Lord. I'm talking about people going from being heroin addicts to entrepreneurs with no addiction problem. I'm talking about real spiritual warfare that produces a tangible reward.

David didn't kill an invisible Goliath. He took out an actual flesh-and-blood Goliath and gained a tax-exempt status for life, along with the king's daughter as a wife. I hesitated to use the words *spiritual warfare* in the title because the last thing I want is for you to imagine yourself atop the highest point in your city, barefoot, playing the acoustic guitar over the city. If it doesn't have a tangible reward, then it's fake.

Here's an example of what I mean by real battles. I know a pastor in another country who had the largest church on the continent. The government did not like that he had such a large church, so they tried to take him out. He was a man of African nationality who relocated to Europe. For years, they tried to deport him to his former European home and kick him out of the country. When that plan failed, they launched an eminent domain action to seize his church's property.

When they take your property through eminent domain, they must give you property of equal or greater value. So they gave him more church property, but it was on the opposite side of the city. It was the equivalent of New York seizing a church in Brooklyn and replacing the land they took with property on Staten Island. It turned a short commute into an hour and 40-minute drive to church—people stopped coming.

That's an actual attack: land seizures, lawsuits, and devilish harassment that disrupt your dream and destiny. This book will show you how to prevail in such attacks one hundred percent of the time.

1

VICTORY BELONGS TO YOU

"Moses my servant is dead. Therefore, the time has come for you to lead these people, the Israelites, across the Jordan River into the land I am giving them. I promise you what I promised Moses: 'Wherever you set foot, you will be on land I have given you—from the Negev wilderness in the south to the Lebanon mountains in the north, from the Euphrates River in the east to the Mediterranean Sea in the west, including all the land of the Hittites.' No one will be able to stand against you as long as you live. For I will be with you as I was with Moses. I will not fail you or abandon you."

— JOSHUA 1:2-5

He didn't say no one would try, but God has given you a guarantee that every time somebody rises against you, they will not succeed. When the Israelites suffered their first defeat against a town called Ai, Joshua threw himself on the ground and wanted to know what was wrong. He didn't say, "Well, we've won six battles straight. It makes sense that we'd lose one...can't win forever." He took God's words literally. When God told him no one would beat him, Joshua knew the only way he could suffer defeat was if there was a problem on his end. The problem was sin. Sin had opened the door for the enemy to defeat Joshua and the Israelites. If Joshua were a modern Christian, he would've just said, "Well, we won a lot, can't win them all. Sometimes things go right, sometimes things go wrong, mountains and valleys..."

Joshua chapter one shows you that victory belongs to you personally. You don't have to try to get victory because victory is not your ambition. Victory is your birthright in Christ. God has ordained you to prevail in every battle of life. That's a big shift in mindset for many people. You're not trying to get something that's not yours. The outcome is not up for grabs. No one will be able to prevail against you as long as you live. *"Only then will you prosper and succeed in all you do"* (Joshua 1:8). Victory, success, and prosperity are not your ambition; they are your birthright.

Remember, no man takes his promised land unchallenged. In Deuteronomy 2:24, God says, *"I've given you the land. Now engage him in battle and begin to possess it."* When God gives you something, engage in the battle and possess what God said is yours. Many people miss it because they mistake opposition for defeat. Never mistake opposition for defeat. Never mistake a challenge for defeat. It's normal to have opposition, but it's unscriptural to be defeated. That's where many believers miss it.

Once you discover the will of God for your life, you have to rise up against anything that opposes you.

As soon as most believers are confronted with opposition, they back down. They believe there won't be any opposition if something is God's will.

No man takes his promised land uncontested. Never mistake a challenge for a defeat. People will rise against you, saying, "As long as I'm in charge of this, you're never going to have what you ask for." They don't have the power to do that. If God is for you, who can be against you? You're not trying to get something that doesn't belong to you. You're not fighting for victory. You're fighting from a position of victory because you already have victory.

God told Joshua, "I've given you the land of that king. Engage him in battle and begin to possess it." That king could have told Moses, "Listen, I legally own this land. As long as I'm here, you'll never have it." From a natural standpoint, he wouldn't be wrong. But God said, "I've already ordained you to have it. Now go engage him in battle. He's not going to give it to you. Go lock it up with him and get it."

Fighting from a position of victory means the outcome is foreordained. You have the victory. Whatever you need to sort out, whoever rises against you, deal with them. Engage them in battle. Don't hide. Don't simply hope it goes away. Whatever you don't confront, you'll never conquer. What you refuse to confront will remain unconquered.

God called Lester Sumrall to preach and start a church in South Bend, Indiana. The building was immediately too small, so they bought land to build a more suitable church building. The mayor of South Bend, Indiana, back in the '70s, received seventy-three letters from surrounding landowners disputing whether they could clear trees from the property. "That's the home of the squirrels. There are a lot of great animals that live there." Seventy-three people signed a petition to stop Lester Sumrall from building this church on the land he owned. The town denied the building permit. He couldn't build there—so they said.

Lester Sumrall entered the mayor's office without an appointment, walked in, and sat on the mayor's side of the desk. He told the mayor he had heard about the 73 people who signed a petition to stop him from building a church on his land. He told the mayor that he had a thousand families in his church and threatened to bring them all downtown with signs, until he wished he'd been elected dogcatcher if he didn't get his permit. He got the permit in less than 15 minutes.

 Engage in battle, begin to possess it. What you don't confront, you won't conquer.

John G. Lake often said, "People use prayer to dodge the action of faith." Lester Sumrall didn't stay in his bedroom praying, "Lord, speak to the mayor's heart." No, Lester Sumrall needed to speak to the Mayor's heart. The Mayor might not be saved, so he can't hear the voice of God, anyway. He had to talk to him. What you don't confront, you'll never conquer. You have victory, but victory must be enforced.

God gave the Promised Land to Israel, but they had to fight to possess it. Once they took possession of it, they had to fight to keep it. You win your battle to take ground. Then, your opposition regroups and tries to come back in and take it. The forefathers of America knew that. That's why, in response to whether America was a republic or a monarchy, Benjamin Franklin said, "A Republic, if you can keep it." He didn't say, "Wow, we drove the British out. We've set up America. Now everything is going to be fine." No, he knew there would be future battles. The enemy would regroup and try to take the freedom America had just won.

You must fight to take what God has already given you. God gave you the power to prevail in every battle of life. Your success and your victory are not up for grabs. It's guaranteed if you take the proper steps. Remember, God promised to make you the head, not the tail; above, never beneath (Deuteronomy 28:13).

You will always be on top. You'll never be at the bottom. You never have to lose a battle. Never. It's not ups and downs; it's ups and ups, from glory to glory, victory to victory, and strength to strength. The last battle you ever lost can be the last battle you ever lose.

2
POWERFUL ENEMIES PRODUCE EVEN MORE POWERFUL FRIENDS

As Saul watched David go out to fight the Philistine, he asked
Abner, the commander of his army, "Abner, whose son is
this young man?"
"I really don't know," Abner declared.
"Well, find out who he is!" the king told him.
As soon as David returned from killing Goliath, Abner
brought him to Saul with the Philistine's head still in his
hand. "Tell me about your father, young man," Saul said.
And David replied, "His name is Jesse, and we live in
Bethlehem."

— 1 SAMUEL 17:55-58

Goliath had the reputation of a mighty soldier. When David faced Goliath, it united the army's top leaders, including the five-star general Abner and King Saul, with David. David was an unknown and the least prominent in his family. It was similar to a worker in a fast-food restaurant having a meeting with the President of the United States.

People often avoid fighting because they recognize their opposition. The more powerful your enemy is, the more powerful friends you'll attract when confronting that enemy. People are watching from the shadows. They observe. They're quiet. Your enemy is loud, but there are a lot of quiet observers. *"For I am with you, and no one will attack and harm you, for many people in this city belong to me"* (Acts 18:10).

The way some people talk, you'd think everybody's against them. The Devil's discouraged them into believing that. If what they say is true, something is very wrong.

God essentially told Paul, "I know you're discouraged, but relax. One, I won't let anybody successfully attack you, and two, many in this city belong to me." Allies are waiting behind the scenes. When David fled from Saul, 600 men joined him. When you make your move, others will join you.

Another example is when I held a crusade and the city government didn't want me there. They turned against me. We had numerous death threats, enough that the Department of Homeland Security came to oversee the first night of the crusade. When I talk about opposition and warfare, know that I've been through a thing or two. Not a ton, but a thing or two.

Despite those who tried to stop or threaten me, we still had the crusade—we stood our ground. After the crusade, a high-powered lawyer called me. He wasn't a Christian; he just wanted to fight against injustice. I spoke graciously. I didn't know who he was, but I talked to him. It turns out he had significant connections as a powerful attorney. He explained that to hold the counter-demonstration against my crusade, permits had to be applied for at least 30 days in advance. How did they obtain one in five days? Illegally. They also weren't charged a permit fee for their demonstration, yet they charged me a high permit fee. That's also illegal. This lawyer sued the city for discrimination on my behalf.

This attorney had been watching me get bullied from a distance. It felt like we had nobody on our side, but people with power were watching. If you conduct yourself right, God will anoint people to fight on your behalf.

I can't make this claim for every country, but in America, we don't like seeing anybody get bullied. If you're in a situation where powerful people are conspiring against you—attempting to take you out—people notice and are quick to do something about it. Sometimes, you'll discover problems were cleared up before you ever knew a thing about it.

Americans don't like bullies, and Americans root for underdogs. That's why *Rocky* is one of the most popular films ever. Americans don't root for the rich heavyweight champion with all the money. They root for the poor guy who trained daily to take him out. America runs in a cycle. They build people up, and when they get to the top, they move to take them down. Then, once they're back at the bottom, they root for them because they're the underdog again.

Have you ever noticed that? There's something about this country that compels people to fight for underdogs. If you feel like an underdog, it's an advantage. But be careful once you become the overdog because people will treat you differently.

Most of you know of Joel Osteen. When his father, John Osteen, wanted to buy the Compaq Center—the former home of the Houston Rockets—influential people told him he'd never get that arena for his church. Arenas are often a city's most valuable revenue source. If a church buys it, the city loses out on the tax revenue. When Houston's power players opposed John Osteen, it brought other influential Texans to his aid and caused Osteen to prevail.

Your enemy has enemies. You might not know who they are, but your enemy has enemies. When you stand toe to toe with your adversary, the enemies of your enemy become eager to help.

The attorney who helped me with my crusade was eager to do so because the city had caused him problems. He was eager to sue them on behalf of someone treated unfairly. When you engage your enemy, you'll attract powerful allies.

When you confront opposition, don't think you're doing it alone. Not only do you have the Lord on your side, but some people don't like to see others bullied and don't like the person you're up against. They may have no affinity for you other than wanting an opportunity to stick it to their old foe, so they'll back you.

It's not about looking for people to attack without reason, it's about coming against those who oppose you. The art of spiritual warfare is about fighting life's battles and coming out victorious.

The art of spiritual warfare can be applied to business as well. A man who owned a tow truck business asked me to pray for his business to expand. I prayed for him, and God indeed expanded his tow truck business. Then, he received a call from a biker gang member, saying he had three days to stop his operation or they would put him out of business. When a biker gang tells you they're going to put you out of business, they don't mean they'll give you a lot of bad reviews on Yelp or file negative reports with the Better Business Bureau. They usually mean you're going to disappear without a trace. His business expanded to the point where it was taking business from competitors, and these particular competitors had their own creative ways of dealing with competition.

We prayed, and the head of the biker gang called that Christian business owner and said, "It's come to my attention that you're a righteous man. Keep operating your business. You won't have any problems with us." God answered that prayer. Stand your ground.

The Devil allows success to a point. But when you break past certain limits, you will feel it. I wouldn't have any problems if I kept my church attendance around 40 to 60 people. If I purposed to preach two Sundays a month, the Devil would leave me alone. But when you go bigger, you bother the Devil. There are people anointed by Hell to keep you small, and they will show up.

Think of it this way. When an arborist puts trees in a nursery, they wrap their roots to keep them from growing into giant trees where they can't house them anymore. They're put in containers that limit their growth. The spirit world and your nation try to put limits on your growth. You have a choice: stay within the imposed limits and have a nice, peaceful life, or you can bust through that plastic container and grow into a big, strong tree.

The Bible says, *"David triumphed over the Philistine with only a sling and a stone, for he had no sword"* (1 Samuel 17:50). David and Goliath did engage in a skirmish, but David left that battle with no bruises. There was never a hand laid on him. There was no sword in his hand. You can win without a physical fight.

> I look up to the mountains—
> does my help come from there?
> My help comes from the Lord,
> who made heaven and earth!
> He will not let you stumble;
> the one who watches over you will not slumber.
> Indeed, he who watches over Israel
> never slumbers or sleeps.
> The Lord himself watches over you!

The Lord stands beside you as your protective shade.
The sun will not harm you by day,
nor the moon at night.
The Lord keeps you from all harm
and watches over your life.
The Lord keeps watch over you as you come and go,
both now and forever.

— PSALM 121:1-8

The Lord keeps you from all harm. One of the many things I love about God is that He's not an idiot. You don't serve a God who's all love and doesn't understand that there are wicked people in the world. When problems come, you're not alone. God made allowance in the Bible for wicked people, wicked plans, and wicked schemes. God knows some people have never worked a day to accomplish their dream, but they're extra motivated to keep you from achieving your dream. God made allowances for wicked people, like the Hamans of the Bible. The Bible has many scriptures about protection, help, and what to do when you're up against evil plans.

Bishop David Oyedepo said this: "Life is not fun fair, life is warfare." There are forces aligned against your advancement. God created and commanded man to be fruitful and multiply. The Devil knows this and does his best to keep you from fruitfulness and multiplication.

Real spiritual warfare involves the advancement of your business. Some people in the community, whether lawyers, a rival business, local government, regulatory agencies, etc., will conspire to destroy your business. What do you do when you get called into court on false charges? What do you do when you're being falsely accused?

What should you do if someone falsely accuses you to damage your work or business? False accusations, threats, and unreasonable demands are intended to frustrate your efforts.

God said He won't allow the schemes of the wicked to harm you. He'll keep you from all harm. Paul told the church in Thessalonica, "He'll keep you from evil." You're guaranteed to have battles in life. Life shouldn't involve constant fighting, but you will face battles.

God will give you rest from your enemies. But when those seasons arise, when the anointing is on you to advance, and somebody rises against you, how do you prevail? This is the art of spiritual warfare because we fight our battles in the spirit—we wrestle not against flesh and blood.

> Afterward they traveled from town to town across the entire island until finally they reached Paphos, where they met a Jewish sorcerer, a false prophet named Bar-Jesus. He had attached himself to the governor, Sergius Paulus, who was an intelligent man. The governor invited Barnabas and Saul to visit him, for he wanted to hear the word of God. But Elymas, the sorcerer (as his name means in Greek), interfered and urged the governor to pay no attention to what Barnabas and Saul said. He was trying to keep the governor from believing.
>
> — ACTS 13:6-8

In Acts chapter thirteen, Paul and Barnabas arrived to preach the Gospel. They successfully lead the governor to the Lord. Then comes this satanic man, whose only purpose in life was to thwart the work of Paul and Barnabas. You will deal with people like this in your life, people who don't want to see you advance or who will go to great lengths to keep you from advancing. If you're going to win your battles, you need to have a mind to do it. You can't have a defeated mentality, a discouraged mindset, or an I-have-to-do-what-I'm-told mindset. If the Lord gives you an objective, you must accomplish the objective.

3

THERE IS A BLESSING FOR PERSECUTION

"God blesses those who are persecuted for doing right, for the
Kingdom of Heaven is theirs.
God blesses you when people mock you and persecute you
and lie about you and say all sorts of evil things against
you because you are my followers. Be happy about it! Be
very glad! For a great reward awaits you in heaven. And
remember, the ancient prophets were persecuted in the
same way."

— MATTHEW 5:10-12

In February 2020, given the choice to have everything in his
ministry remain the same or be arrested for holding church in
defiance of the lockdown, Pastor Rodney Howard-Browne—and
anyone else in their right mind—would have chosen to stay the
same. However, I bet if you gave Pastor Rodney the choice today, he
would choose the path of resistance because there's a blessing for
persecution. Pastor Rodney's world has completely changed since
the day he was arrested. His church has nearly tripled in attendance,

whereas most churches have experienced a two-thirds reduction. He has a brand-new building and has realized significant financial increases personally and within his ministry. There is a blessing for being persecuted for following Jesus.

Jesus said you're blessed when people say all sorts of evil things against you. There's an actual, tangible blessing that comes into your life when you are persecuted for the Kingdom.

When it becomes public that your business gives 10 percent of your revenue to support the Gospel of Jesus Christ—or, as the media would frame it, anti-LGBTQ causes—people start moving against you as they did with Chick-fil-A. The City of San Antonio told Chick-fil-A that they couldn't have a restaurant at the airport. Years prior, the mayor of Boston tried to restrict Chick-fil-A from opening locations in the city. It isn't legal to ban a business from a city because you disagree with their religious views. When these things happen to you, the Bible says God will bless you, assuming you stand and don't cave. That should give you the motivation to stand up. You actually should count it all joy. *"Dear brothers and sisters, when troubles of any kind come your way, consider it an opportunity for great joy"* (James 1:2).

The Bible says Jesus endured the shame and indignity of the cross because He knew the joy that was set before Him. There will always be a reward on the other side of your giant. The Devil's attempts to cause trouble aren't without reason. The Devil's purpose for causing trouble is to discourage you from staying where you are. But if you conquer that giant, your life will change for the better.

Imagine if Pastor Rodney had shut his church down or limited it to 25 people. Where would his ministry be today? Whenever you encounter persecution, count it all joy. It's a sign that you're headed toward the blessing. You should be nervous if nothing ever comes against you.

Train yourself to look forward to challenges, knowing your victory is not in question. You should get nervous about persecution only if you believe that man can end your destiny. Your future is not in the hands of the Devil. Your future is not in the hands of man. Your future is in the hands of God when you stay in covenant with Him. *"The Lord keeps you from all harm and watches over your life"* (Psalm 121:7). Don't allow the Devil to convince you that you're going through difficulties alone or that no one understands. God will keep you from all harm, and He's watching over your life. Your victory is certain.

Despite all the threats of arrest and shutdown during COVID, what church in the United States was forcibly shut down? None. They made threats but ultimately could not follow through with them. That's why it's critical to stay in covenant with God. Man doesn't have the power to touch you. Nothing shall, by any means, harm you.

4

YOU MUST DECIDE TODAY

D o you want to remain small with no enemies or large with large enemies?

During the COVID lockdowns, many pastors were secretly glad they only had 19 people in their church because it allowed them to go unnoticed. If your goal is to go unnoticed, you won't have any problems—mission accomplished. But since God anointed us to multiply and be prominent in business and ministry, you have a decision to make. Are you going to remain small and unremarkable or advance and deal with the assaults that come along with having an influential business, church, ministry, or crusade?

If you're an evangelist, you won't receive much persecution for going out and winning a soul or two or talking to people one-on-one about their faith. But if you attempt to gather 5,000 people to hear the Gospel in your city, you'll meet some people in local government you've never met before—people who aren't your friends, who hate the Gospel, hate you and everything you do.

"Why do you have to do this here? Why do you need that many people to come?" they'll ask. Those questions are never asked of their hockey or football teams. "Why do they need that many people to come to the stadium? Why do they have to make all that noise?" The issue is not between them and you. The problem is between them and God. They hate God and the name of Jesus. Jesus isn't available for them to yell at, so they yell at you instead. When you take abuse on behalf of God, He gives you His blessing. Decide today whether you want to be small with no enemies or large with many enemies. Settle it in your mind.

Growth is not your ambition; it's your birthright through redemption. There's a blessing on your life for multiplication. The enemy may create some problems in the short term, but he has no power to derail you. Get a long-term view. Don't make decisions that bring comfort today and no growth tomorrow. Make decisions that are uncomfortable right now, but bring multiplication. Don't work to stand before Jesus and hand His talent back to Him.

At the beginning of the COVID lockdown, I received a letter from a church where I was scheduled to speak that read, "I don't want you to come to my church. I've heard you're holding services during the pandemic. It would be best if you thought about what you're doing. You're not using wisdom. You're going to bring shame and reproach to the body of Christ." Over two years later, that guy's church is going under because he shut down, and people aren't coming anymore. Meanwhile, our ministry has tripled since COVID.

Christians mistakenly think the path of least resistance is the path God intends for them. It's not. Never let anything deter you from your objective. Wise choices produce an increase; poor choices bring a decrease.

Being careful will kill your business, and it will destroy your ministry. The Bible says to be careful for nothing. We're not careful people; we're aggressive people. I take risks. If I wanted to be careful, I'd quit the ministry. Jesus told us what to expect as Christians in this age. He told us that we'll be dragged into courts because we're His followers. For those who interpret Romans chapter thirteen to mean you're always to obey the government, how would you explain Jesus telling us we will get dragged into court for being a follower of Christ?

In 1 Samuel chapter seventeen, we see that the anointing on your life will attract enemies. The greater the anointing, the greater the enemies, as we see in the life of David.

If you're a minister in Canada, your ministry can carry an anointing strong enough to trouble the city government. But there can come a time when the anointing on your ministry increases to the point where it angers the provincial government. Then, the time might come when your ministry has an anointing so great it reaches and changes the nation and attracts the national government's attention. You can tell how big your anointing is by the enemies you attract.

When we held a crusade in New Jersey, multiple city governments moved against me to shut down the crusade. I got a call from an older preacher saying, "You should be encouraged." I thought, 'Well, I'm not. This is ticking me off.'

He said, "I heard the city met to shut your meeting down."

"They did," I replied.

"Well, that says you have an anointing strong enough to shake that city."

If the attorney general of the United States gets involved, you have an anointing strong enough to shake the nation. Local anointing, local enemies. Regional anointing, regional enemies. National anointing, national enemies. Global anointing, global enemies.

The anointing on your life attracts opposition. Big things attract enemies. That's why most people, without realizing it, have built small churches, small businesses, small evangelistic meetings, and small outreaches.

I've had two churches contact me, saying they're planning a small outreach and asking me to come and preach. My answer is no. I'm not interested in small outreaches. Get a small preacher to do a small outreach. I'm not interested in doing small things. You don't need faith for small things. You don't need God for small things. You can do small things with human strength.

If you call me up and say, "Our small church is tired of being small. We're planning a big outreach. We're believing for 2,000 souls to be saved in a week," you'll have my attention. You'll probably have more trouble paying for a small outreach than a large one. People don't realize it, but they subconsciously decide to be small.

Do you want to be small with no enemies or large with big enemies? Make up your mind. Some people have never worked a single day in their lives toward building their dreams, but they've devoted their entire lives to destroying the dreams of others. I don't know why this is true, but it is, and God will deal with those people.

Haman's life mission had nothing to do with his own life. He had no dream other than to kill the Jews—not a great dream. God dealt with him. Haman hung on a gallows built for his enemies.

5

LIVE RIGHTEOUSLY

The wicked run away when no one is chasing them, but the godly are as bold as lions.

— PROVERBS 28:1

A righteous life produces boldness.

Have you ever wondered why people with national ministries didn't take a stand against COVID lockdowns? They seemed like strong leaders. I was shocked that they hid and shut their churches down. Why would an established, strong leader cower in this manner? There was no way the government could have successfully stood against them, but they never challenged the government. Then, things came out two years later. There were problems in the shadows of their ministry's organization. Alcohol problems and other addictions created legal issues. Matters that were hidden are now exposed.

If you go to war, you better live clean because all your secrets will be exposed during battle. If you have skeletons in your closet, they'll all come out. If you intend to engage in a spiritual battle, you better live a righteous life. Righteousness produces boldness. Sin produces cowardice. Righteousness makes you bold because you can say things like Jesus said, *"The prince of this world is coming for me, but he has nothing in me"* (John 14:30). Satan can rage all he wants, but he cannot do anything to me without sin in my life.

Do you know how often I've heard ministers say, "You need to be careful what you say when you preach because the way you preach, you're going to get audited by the IRS"? Go ahead and audit me. Send an accountant to look at my books. They're in order, and I have no concerns.

Conduct your life, ministry, and business in a manner that enables you to go to war. Always be prepared for a spiritual battle, because if you're not, you will bow your knee to Baal when the music is played. The only way to stand boldly and fight is to live a righteous life. When you live righteously, boldness is as natural as breathing—you don't have to try to be bold, you are bold.

Righteousness produces boldness. Sin produces cowardice. Righteousness is ingredient number one when engaging in spiritual warfare.

> Oh, the joys of those who do not follow the advice of the wicked, or stand around with sinners, or join in with mockers.
> But they delight in the law of the Lord, meditating on it day and night.
> They are like trees planted along the riverbank, bearing fruit each season.
> Their leaves never wither, and they prosper in all they do.
>
> — PSALM 1:1-3

Where you stand, where you sit, and whom you walk with matters in life. There are certain places I don't go. There are certain things I won't do because I'm a Christian. I live righteously. You never know when a battle is coming.

6

YOUR ENEMY WILL MAKE
MISTAKES

Haman, however, stayed behind to plead for his life with
Queen Esther, for he knew that the king intended to kill
him. In despair he fell on the couch where Queen Esther
was reclining, just as the king was returning from the
palace garden.

The king exclaimed, "Will he even assault the queen right here
in the palace, before my very eyes?" And as soon as the
king spoke, his attendants covered Haman's face, signaling
his doom.

— ESTHER 7:7-8

Your enemy will make mistakes.

Just as the children of God are anointed to prevail, the
enemies of the children of God are anointed to make mistakes. Sit
back and wait for your enemy to make a mistake—it's guaranteed to
happen. They will file the paperwork improperly. In their eagerness
to shut your business down, they'll make illegal moves against it. It

will come to light, and you can put the screws to them. Wait for it. I'm not suggesting your enemies *might* make a mistake; I'm telling you they *will* make a mistake. They'll do something in secret that comes out against them.

As with Haman, in the book of Esther, your enemy will make a fatal mistake. It's not like Haman failed in his mission to destroy the Jews, and Esther was allowed to live, and he was sad. Haman made a mistake and took himself out. I'm not suggesting you attack people, but you do this when someone attacks you. Be as harmless as doves, but as wise as a serpent.

This is what happens when an enemy attacks a righteous man. My friend pastors a church, and a lady showed up at his church with her lawyers in tow. She claimed her son was molested at his church. It turned out her son was 19, and he slept with another man who happened to be an occasional volunteer at that church. Two grown men being together is not molestation. The lady's son is gay and chose to sleep with another man. That's not the pastor's fault. But she made the accusation through her lawyers and threatened to sue.

The church's lawyers told my friend it was best to settle to avoid bringing bad publicity to the church. They advised him against defending himself in court because the legal cost to defend the case would be quite high.

Instead of listening to the *experts*, my friend looked directly at the woman threatening to sue him and said, "Let me tell you something, lady. I'll gladly spend 2 million dollars to ensure you don't get one dollar." That lady's attorney raised his eyebrows, the church's attorney raised his eyebrows, she raised her eyebrows, and the suit was dropped.

People may think you're a pushover, but when you show them that you can't be pushed around, they'll look for another target. The

Devil attacks soft targets. He doesn't like to fight because he's terrible at fighting. He's never won a fight...he's a bum.

When somebody punches, punch back. Your enemy will always make a mistake.

 The time has come for me to lead.

Your time is now. God didn't make a mistake putting you on the Earth in this hour. Don't develop the mindset that things would be better if you were born in a different time. Don't delay, hoping things will change. Don't blame current leaders for problems or look to new ones for relief. Are you going to paralyze yourself for four years because the government is unfriendly or incompetent? No, *now* is your time.

One of the great messages of the Bible is that if you partner with God, He has the power to override every obstacle in your path. That's what I'm trying to get into your spirit. Don't look at what other people are planning against you. Some people are paralyzed because of perceived or actual threats against their business or ministry. People in their mid-sixties wait for their mother to die to collect their inheritance and begin life. Don't live in fear and miss your whole life. The time is now.

When Joshua was mourning Moses, God told him,

> "Moses my servant is dead. Therefore, the time has come for
> you to lead these people, the Israelites, across the Jordan
> River into the land I am giving them. I promise you what I
> promised Moses: 'Wherever you set foot, you will be on
> land I have given you—from the Negev wilderness in the
> south to the Lebanon mountains in the north, from the
> Euphrates River in the east to the Mediterranean Sea in

the west, including all the land of the Hittites. No one will be able to stand against you as long as you live. For I will be with you as I was with Moses. I will not fail you or abandon you."

— JOSHUA 1:2-5

This is an appropriate portion of Scripture to read to the United Nations. They need to understand that the land the Israelis are in—that the Jewish people are in—was not stolen. It's the land that God gave by covenant to Abraham and Moses. If you try to move them out of there, best of luck to you.

I read an interview with a Hamas leader—some call them soldiers, and some call them terrorists. He explained his interactions with the Israeli-developed Iron Dome system. Hamas fires missiles into Israel, and the Iron Dome blasts the missiles out of the air with laser precision. When Hamas launches missiles into Israel, they don't even bother to cancel school; they blow every missile out of the sky. The Daily Mail, which is not a Christian publication, reported, "An Israeli Iron Dome operator is claiming that he witnessed 'the hand of God' diverting an incoming Hamas missile into the sea." Hamas leaders might want to wise up and realize they're fighting a losing cause.

God made a covenant with Abraham, Moses, and Joshua. A key Scripture in the Bible is Acts 10:34, which says that God is no respecter of persons. God doesn't arbitrarily choose who He's going to bless. He doesn't respect you based on who your mother is or based on your level of education. How does God decide whom He's going to put His hand upon? There's only one way to gain God's attention—faith, believing what God said.

You're also free to decide not to believe the Bible. Some people have no time for The Bible. They think it's something to encourage you through hard times, but it's much more. It's God's covenant with man. He tells you what to do, and if you do what He says, He does what He said He'll do. *"I'll give you good success. No man will be able to stand against you as long as you live"* (Joshua 1:8). These are promises from God. If you do what He tells you to do, no man will be able to stand against you as long as you live. It doesn't say they won't try. That's what leads many people to defeat. Never confuse an enemy or a challenge with defeat. God wouldn't have written that scripture unless there was a tendency for people to stand against you.

Some people have never been motivated to do anything to build their success. But when they witness someone else achieve success, it's as if a demon jumps on them, and they become highly motivated to stop that person's advancement. There's a scripture in the book of Nehemiah found in the Old Testament, where God directs Nehemiah to rebuild the wall of Jerusalem. As soon as he began rebuilding the Jerusalem wall, Sanballat and Tobiah did everything they could to shut him down. They had no goals for their own life.

The same thing happens today. The Bible shows the timelessness of human nature and the Devil's tactics. There are people with no goals other than to see you fail, take your wealth, the thing you built, or destroy your success. Thankfully, God is not an idiot. He made provision for this kind of behavior. Though people try to stop you, He said nobody will ever stand against you successfully when you persevere. You can choose to quit, but if you don't give up, God will help you prevail in every battle of life.

7

PROPHESY YOUR VICTORY, NOT THE JUDGMENTS OF YOUR ENEMIES

Never repeat negative verdicts spoken against you. Very few, if any, sentences should begin with "they said."

"They said we can't—we're not going to be able."

They might have said it, but don't repeat it. Death and life are in the power of the tongue. Say the opposite. Say what God said: "I'll prosper and succeed in everything I do."

"They said they're going to shut us down."

No. We're going to multiply. We're blessed, and we're multiplied. Don't use your mouth to speak the judgments of your enemies.

How often does the Bible say, *"Thus saith the Lord"*? Say what God said, not what your enemies say.

Everyone talked about famine in 2 Kings chapter seven, but Elisha said, *"Thus saith the Lord, by this time tomorrow, food will be cheaper than before this siege hit the land"* (2 Kings 7:1).

Prophesy your victory, not the judgments of your enemy.

8

KEEP YOUR JOY AND STRENGTH

The joy of the Lord is your strength!

— NEHEMIAH 8:10

I f you keep your joy, you'll keep your strength.

If someone served you with a lawsuit in an attempt to shut down your business, God would give you a plan. You would receive instructions and obtain the right attorney. Everything would go smoothly, and you'd win your lawsuit. Then, you'd counter-sue for defamation or abuse of process, win that case, and get your court fees back.

But if for the 14 months it took to win your case, you were nervous, unable to sleep at night, and constantly anxious, though you won legally, you really lost. You probably developed stomach ulcers and health problems because stress is a doorway to sickness and disease. It's important to win and maintain your joy throughout the battle.

What good is it to withstand a challenge if it causes problems in your marriage because you were harsh with your wife and children? If you're confident that the Lord will deliver your enemies into your hands, allow it to reflect in your personality. People around you should have no idea you're facing a challenge—unlike nearly everybody else in our generation.

 I will maintain my joy through the battle.

Norm Macdonald is a perfect example of this concept. He's a comedian who recently passed away. He died after a nine-year battle with cancer, and no one knew he was even sick. He felt it would have affected whether people laughed at his shows because if everyone knew he had cancer, they would feel bad for him. No one found out he had cancer until after he died.

People shouldn't know about the challenges you're facing. Keep it between you and God. Telling other people is a sign that you're still worried about it. People should find out what you went through and say, "Are you sure? I was just with him last week. He said nothing about that. He was telling jokes." That's how you frustrate the Devil because the end goal of the Devil is to use a crisis to destroy your joy and steal your strength.

If, while planning a significant outreach or crusade, you experienced threats and problems and allowed that to worry you throughout the entire process, even if you prevailed, you'd subconsciously avoid outreaches in the future. People don't do things that bring them pain. It's important to remain joyful through the challenge. If you know your victory is secure, why worry about anything? It's unscriptural to worry. The Bible tells you not to worry about anything; instead, pray about everything.

Always be full of joy in the Lord. I say it again—rejoice! Let
everyone see that you are considerate in all you do.
Remember, the Lord is coming soon.
Don't worry about anything; instead, pray about everything.
Tell God what you need, and thank him for all he has
done.

— PHILIPPIANS 4:4-6

The Bible doesn't just *tell* you to be joyful. It *shows* you how to be joyful by giving you the recipe. If anything bothers you, bring it to God and refuse to think about it anymore. Every time the thought of what you prayed about comes back to your mind, say aloud, "I thank You, Father, that You heard my prayer about this matter. Because You've heard me, I know You've answered me. In Jesus' name, I pray, amen." Cast your cares on Him, and then don't have a rope attached so you can pull it back.

 If you allow battles to exhaust you, you'll avoid them even though God's given you the victory.

In mixed martial arts, when the fighters stand beside each other at the end, you can't tell who won if you weren't watching the fight. The guy who lost has his face beaten to shreds. His eyes are swollen, and his face is bleeding. The guy who won also has swollen eyes and a bloody face. He won, but he suffered heavy damage.

A friend of mine won his MMA fight by choking out his opponent in the first minute. He looked as handsome at the end of the fight as in the beginning. I don't believe he ever took a hit. Don't just aim to win the fight. Instead, aim to look handsome at the end.

9

THE BATTLE IS THE LORD'S

C onnect your life to the Kingdom of God. If you try to go it alone, then the battle is all yours to fight.

Is your business tied to the advancement of the Church? If it's not, you're responsible for defending it. God said, *"I will build my church, and the gates of hell will not prevail against it"* (Matthew 16:18). Jesus oversees the advancement of everything tied to His Church. Anything that's not tied to His Church: best of luck. It's up to you.

Your business should be a tithing business. Your ministry should be a tithing ministry. I don't mean that it's a ministry that teaches tithing. It should be a ministry that sends a tenth of everything that comes in to other preaching ministries, separate from your ministry. Your tithe ensures that God rebukes all devourers for your sake without you even having to pray about it.

The battle is not yours. The battle is the Lord's, assuming you're tied in with Him. Make sure you tithe, and then don't worry. The prince of this world is coming for you, but he can't do anything if he has nothing in you. That's what Jesus said. Holiness ensures Satan can't put his hand on you. Make sure of those two things—tithe and live without sin.

10

CALL YOUR ENEMY'S BLUFF

Goliath walked out toward David with his shield bearer ahead of him, sneering in contempt at this ruddy-faced boy. "Am I a dog," he roared at David, "that you come at me with a stick?" And he cursed David by the names of his gods. "Come over here, and I'll give your flesh to the birds and wild animals!" Goliath yelled.

David replied to the Philistine, "You come to me with sword, spear, and javelin, but I come to you in the name of the Lord of Heaven's Armies—the God of the armies of Israel, whom you have defied. Today the Lord will conquer you, and I will kill you and cut off your head. And then I will give the dead bodies of your men to the birds and wild animals, and the whole world will know that there is a God in Israel! And everyone assembled here will know that the Lord rescues his people, but not with sword and spear. This is the Lord's battle, and he will give you to us!"

As Goliath moved closer to attack, David quickly ran out to meet him. Reaching into his shepherd's bag and taking out a stone, he hurled it with his sling and hit the Philistine in the forehead. The stone sank in, and Goliath stumbled and fell face down on the ground.

So David triumphed over the Philistine with only a sling and a stone, for he had no sword. Then David ran over and pulled Goliath's sword from its sheath. David used it to kill him and cut off his head.

— 1 SAMUEL 17:41-51

W hen someone makes false accusations against you, call their bluff. Force them to make good on their threats. That's what we did through the entire COVID pandemic. I've heard it all. For instance, "If you hold that meeting, it violates the Department of Health directives, we'll shut you down."

My response: "Then come shut us down, but I'm not shutting myself down. So come do it."

They never did.

A friend of mine who pastors a church had the police show up on a Sunday morning to tell him that if he held church the following Sunday, they had orders from the governor to arrest him. His response: "Then be here at 10 o'clock sharp and bring more than one squad car."

They never came back.

Call their bluff, as David did to Goliath. Anybody can talk. Find out whether your enemy can do what they say they can do. Challenge your challengers. The Bible says, *"Every tongue that shall rise against thee in judgment thou shalt condemn"* (Isaiah 54:17). Notice it doesn't say God will condemn; it says *you* will condemn.

When the Devil talks, talk back. Say, "Who do you think you're talking to?" A closed mouth is a closed destiny.

Be like David. He knew he was in covenant with God and his enemy wasn't, so he acted accordingly.

 I'm in covenant with God. My enemy is not in covenant with God. If God is for me, who can be against me?

You're tied in with God. Anything that can't defeat God can't defeat you. Your life is hidden with Christ in God (Colossians 3:3). That's what the Bible says. That means if you're with Christ in God, to get to you, someone has to get through God, the Father.

Be immune to threats from the enemy. If people run their mouths, don't let their words find a home in your head—and don't let them find a home in your heart.

Think of it this way. If you're walking home one day and a four-year-old standing on the sidewalk says, "I'm going to kill you, I'm going to steal your business," what would you do? You'd probably assume the kid was off their medication. You wouldn't think about it for one day. Why? Because they can't do what they're threatening. Guess what? Neither can anybody else. Take their words as seriously as you take the words of a four-year-old child.

11

GIVE GOD ALL THE GLORY

Give Him glory *before* the battle, *during* the battle, and *after* the battle. Praise is a powerful weapon.

"But you will not even need to fight. Take your positions; then
stand still and watch the Lord's victory. He is with you, O
people of Judah and Jerusalem. Do not be afraid or
discouraged. Go out against them tomorrow, for the Lord
is with you!"
Then King Jehoshaphat bowed low with his face to the
ground. And all the people of Judah and Jerusalem did the
same, worshiping the Lord. Then the Levites from the
clans of Kohath and Korah stood to praise the Lord, the
God of Israel, with a very loud shout.

— 2 CHRONICLES 20:17-19

And when they began to sing and to praise, the Lord set
ambushments against the children of Ammon, Moab, and

mount Seir, which were come against Judah; and they were smitten.

— 2 CHRONICLES 20:22 (KJV)

Though the battle is the Lord's, you still have your position and role. Your role is to give God praise. Praise warfare works because, according to Psalm 22:3, God abides in the praises of His people. Angels attend to your prayers—what you're asking for—but God visits your praise. When God steps in, your enemies bow out.

Your success is rooted in your covenant relationship with God. The only way to come into covenant with God the Father is through the blood of His Son, Jesus Christ. If you've never received that sacrifice, you're outside of the covenant with God. You need to know God. He needs to know you. Don't be on the outside looking in.

 I have a significant destiny. My life and destiny are worth fighting for.

Too many people conduct their lives like they're of no significance. They let people take things from them, even take their life. Take your life seriously. If you don't, nobody else will. Reinhard Bonnke used to say, "God doesn't sit with the sitters; He goes with the goers." You can find evidence of that throughout Scripture.

What are you believing for? Where are you headed in life? Why would you let anything stop you from getting there?

Recognize your enemies. You don't keep a rattlesnake in your bed. Likewise, don't hang out with your enemies. Teaching about fighting battles is useless if people can't even recognize they're in one. Once you recognize it, what do you do? You have to fight. But we fight differently. *"The weapons of our warfare are not carnal, but they're mighty"* (2 Corinthians 10:4). We have weapons, but we don't war against flesh and blood.

Life doesn't give you what you deserve; life gives you what you demand. *"...the kingdom of heaven suffereth violence, and the violent take it by force"* (Matthew 11:12).

 I will take it by force.

The Bible says life is but a vapor, here today and gone tomorrow. What are you doing in life? Don't sit around waiting for something to open up; it doesn't work that way. When you start moving forward, God levels your enemies on the path ahead.

> Abishai, the brother of Joab, was the leader of the Thirty. He once used his spear to kill 300 enemy warriors in a single battle. It was by such feats that he became as famous as the Three. Abishai was the most famous of the Thirty and was their commander, though he was not one of the Three.
> There was also Benaiah son of Jehoiada, a valiant warrior from Kabzeel. He did many heroic deeds, which included killing two champions of Moab. Another time, on a snowy day, he chased a lion down into a pit and killed it. Once, armed only with a club, he killed an Egyptian warrior who was 7 1/2 feet tall and who was armed with a spear as thick as a weaver's beam. Benaiah wrenched the spear from the Egyptian's hand and killed him with it. Deeds like these made Benaiah as famous as the three mightiest warriors. He was more honored than the other members of the Thirty, though he was not one of the Three. And David made him captain of his bodyguard.

> — 1 CHRONICLES 11:20-25

Some people think that belief in God means you're supposed to be passive. There's nothing inherently Christian about letting your life be dictated to you. This is especially true if you're watching me from the United States of America or living under a representative government.

The mentality of the Bible didn't change from the Old and New Testaments. The only difference is that we don't physically defeat our enemies. You don't find out who's causing you a problem or who's suing your business and take them out physically. You do it through prayer, and God has given you spiritual equipment. It's not a cop-out or timidity; it works better.

A great preacher from Nigeria started 9,600 churches in his lifetime. When he was born in Nigeria, there were less than 400 churches. He was a mighty man of God. He accomplished all that under an Islamic jihadist dictatorship. He had a saying that when you're challenged, whatever you don't confront, you won't conquer. The title of that message was "Win Without Fighting."

 I can win without fighting.

God gives us the means to win battles without fighting, but you must take your position.

12

THE REWARD IS GREATER THAN THE SACRIFICE

Think about why you are being attacked. People who don't have any problems in life aren't going anywhere. If you don't have enemies, you're living a life that doesn't bother anyone. You're not buying real estate. Your business is not expanding. But if your business grows, it's probably taking business away from somebody else. Your competitor will start talking to their buddy on the council or permit board and begin taking steps to see you shut down. Why would they do that? What's their motivation?

The Devil doesn't attack people who aren't moving forward. His goal is to get you to settle down and accept less. Suppose the Devil sees you're about to hit a breakthrough that will take your business from $100,000 to $1.2 million annually. If you're living righteously, the Devil won't give up any ground. He knows your money will not flow into wine and cigar parties. You're going to use your money to strengthen the will of God on the Earth—feed the hungry, strengthen families, and build churches. When the Devil knows you will do that, he tries to discourage you through obstacles.

You're not fighting for the sake of fighting. There's a reward and a blessing on the other side.

In 1 Samuel chapter seventeen, David was no dummy. He didn't just go out and fight Goliath without thinking. He wanted to know the reward for killing the Philistine. He was told King Saul would grant whoever killed the giant a tax exemption for life. David didn't fight for free; he had his eye on a lifetime tax exemption and the king's daughter. The Bible says that David first confirmed the reward with someone else before challenging Goliath.

 Never fight for free.

If you're going to engage in something, what's the point? What's the reward on the other side? If you're in business, God puts tools in your hand. That money you make becomes a weapon to establish God's will on the Earth. If you're in business, you should never let the words "We have a small business" come out of your mouth, even if it is a small business. I'm not saying you should lie, but you shouldn't see what God gave you as a small thing. You should see a vision of its future and never confess it as small. You can say, "We're starting, but I'm not staying where I'm at." Don't mind where you are right now. Look where you're going and eliminate things blocking your increase.

The first command God gave to man in Genesis 1:28 was *"Be fruitful and multiply."* The things limiting your ability to be fruitful and multiply are not from God. God is for you; He's not against you. He wants to help you multiply. It's important to settle this in your spirit because if you think God's against you, it will take the fight out of you. You won't fight if you think your Father is against you. You'll feel powerless.

You must get it straight in your head. You have an enemy that the Bible calls the Devil, who goes about like a roaring lion, seeking whom he may devour (1 Peter 5:8). He is interested in you staying small, your marriage falling apart, and your kids getting into drugs. That's not God. God is not up in Heaven throwing you random tests.

As a father, I don't wake up and think, 'How can I make my daughter's life difficult today to make her a stronger person?' No, I'll make her a stronger person by instruction, by being a role model, and by example. That's God's way. God doesn't teach by destruction. God teaches by instruction. *"O how love I thy law! it is my meditation all the day. Thou through thy commandments hast made me wiser than mine enemies: for they are ever with me"* (Psalms 119:97-99).

It's not God harming you. James chapter one says every good and perfect gift comes from the Father of lights in whom there is no variance. That means He never changes, nor is there any shadow of turning in Him.

God is a good God and the Devil is a bad devil. When somebody who wants to help you comes into your life, that's the Lord.

After David killed Goliath, he became a national hero. The confrontation is worth having. You'll have people give you advice in business and the ministry. Don't ever get shortsighted, focusing on short-term consequences. Get your eyes on the end goal and keep going forward. Don't take advice from people who are protecting their interests. Remember your goal and your dream, and keep moving toward it.

13
THE PRINCIPLE OF FAITH IS AS PURE GOLD

In the book of James, the Bible says that when you're tested, God does it so your faith will emerge like gold refined in the fire. That's the purpose of trials.

I don't believe any differently about healing or God's protection right now than I did in 2018 before COVID hit. But COVID forced me to make decisions and have thoughts like anybody would have. It made me think, 'If I keep my ministry open and preach and I get COVID and die, I'm going to bring disgrace to the Gospel.' Other ministers told me, "You'll make us all look bad. You need to be careful. I'd lay low if I were you." I had to deal with those thoughts. But I decided that if the promises of protection from all sickness and disease don't work, I'd rather find out now.

I don't believe anything differently now, but I believe it better than ever. I always believed it. Now, I *really* believe it because I've proved it. It was a theory I held. Now, it's a proven fact in my life. Whether I prove it or not, the Word of God is factual, but it becomes a part of you when you prove it. It's like when you start tithing and giving offerings; you believe it or want to do it, but when the reward comes, nobody can talk you out of it.

If I were in a meeting where they refused to receive tithes and offerings, I'd shove the usher aside and lay my money on the altar. My faith in that area is like gold, refined in the fire. It's the same with protection now.

Trials don't give you faith. Trials purify your faith.

In the words of David: *"The Lord that delivered me out of the paw of the lion, and out of the paw of the bear He will deliver me from the hand of this Philistine"* (1 Samuel 17:37). Once you're battle-proven, you have no fear. There's no unbelief to take authority over. You've proved what you believe. Whatever you're going through right now will purify your faith—like pure gold.

1 4

THE WEAPON OF FASTING AND PRAYER

Just then a hand touched me and lifted me, still trembling, to my hands and knees. And the man said to me, "Daniel, you are very precious to God, so listen carefully to what I have to say to you. Stand up, for I have been sent to you." When he said this to me, I stood up, still trembling.

Then he said, "Don't be afraid, Daniel. Since the first day you began to pray for understanding and to humble yourself before your God, your request has been heard in heaven. I have come in answer to your prayer. But for twenty-one days the spirit prince of the kingdom of Persia blocked my way. Then Michael, one of the archangels, came to help me, and I left him there with the spirit prince of the kingdom of Persia. Now I am here to explain what will happen to your people in the future, for this vision concerns a time yet to come."

— DANIEL 10:10-14

Daniel was not on a 21-day fast. He was on a fast until he got his answer. God was not withholding His answer. Before answering, God wasn't waiting to see if Daniel could go without eating for 21 days. There was a demonic principality holding up Daniel's answer. But on the 21st day of prayer and fasting, more angelic help was released to deal with that spirit, and the angel came with his answer.

Fasting and prayer are tremendous weapons. People battle things for 30 years that could have been beaten with three days of fasting and prayer. Few enemies can withstand three days of fasting and prayer.

When it comes to wealth and riches, if you don't sow, you can fast and pray for a hundred days, and you'll still be broke and starve to death. Fasting and prayer can't take the place of sowing and reaping. You can't fast and pray instead of obeying God's Word. But when it comes to an enemy, a demonic thing assailing your life, ministry, or business, very few things can withstand three days of fasting and prayer. Nothing can withstand 21 days of fasting and prayer. Few things can withstand three days of fasting in prayer.

> Then all the Israelites went up to Bethel and wept in the pres-
> ence of the Lord and fasted until evening. They also
> brought burnt offerings and peace offerings to the Lord.
> The Israelites went up seeking direction from the Lord.
> (In those days the Ark of the Covenant of God was in
> Bethel, and Phinehas son of Eleazar and grandson of
> Aaron was the priest.) The Israelites asked the Lord,
> "Should we fight against our relatives from Benjamin
> again, or should we stop?"
> The Lord said, "Go! Tomorrow I will hand them over to you."
>
> — JUDGES 20:26-28

Fasting and prayer are weapons that destroy your enemies.

In 2 Chronicles chapter twenty, the people fasted, and the Lord gave them direction and destroyed their enemies. Fasting and prayer place a kind of invincibility in you. Daniel prayed and fasted all the time. In Daniel chapter ten, they threw him into a lion's den. Unlike David, Daniel didn't have to kill the lion because the lion wouldn't even touch him. Fasting and prayer keep lions from touching you because lions don't eat other lions.

Fasting and prayer—as we see in Judges, chapter twenty; Daniel, chapter ten; and Acts, chapter thirteen—gives divine direction for moving forward. In 2 Chronicles chapter twenty, fasting and prayer caused the Lord to set ambushments against their enemies.

When going through something difficult, you often don't feel like eating anyway, so it's natural to fast during such times.

> Then your salvation will come like the dawn, and your
>   wounds will quickly heal.
> Your godliness will lead you forward, and the glory of the
>   Lord will protect you from behind.
> Then when you call, the Lord will answer.
> 'Yes, I am here,' he will quickly reply.
> "Remove the heavy yoke of oppression.
> Stop pointing your finger and spreading vicious rumors!
>
> — ISAIAH 58:8-9

There are a ton of blessings you receive from fasting. The glory of the Lord will be your rear guard and looses angels to help you.

In 2 Chronicles, chapter twenty, we read that the people fasted, prayed, and praised, and the Lord sent ambushments against their enemies. If you're in a battle and you've not fasted and prayed, you're not serious about winning. If it doesn't mean enough for you to skip two meals, I don't want to hear your tearful story about how much it's bothering you. I don't believe you. You can find numerous scriptures in the Bible where someone received terrible news, tore their clothes, put on sackcloth and ashes, and fasted—I believe them.

Fasting and prayer are not only the greatest weapons of spiritual warfare but also essential weapons. You're fighting with an unloaded gun if you ignore fasting and prayer.

15

IN THE MULTITUDE OF COUNSELORS, THERE'S WISDOM

Without counsel purposes are disappointed: but in the multitude of counsellors they are established.

— PROVERBS 15:22 (KJV)

A secret to success is the wisdom of multiple counselors. Plans fail when there's no counsel but succeed when many wise men are asked for counsel.

Consult wise people, not just one, but many. It's impossible to get discouraged when you have a path forward. You get discouraged and defeated when you don't see a way forward. If you don't know what to do, you haven't talked to wise people. Get advice from people who have already conquered the giant you're facing.

What if you had to fight Goliath but could call David on your cell phone? "Hey David, tomorrow, I'm confronting Goliath. He's either going to kill me, or I will kill him. What should I do?"

He'd probably say something like, "First, don't come at him with a sword, shield, or spear. That's what he's used to."

In the same way that David didn't take advice from King Saul, who had never fought a giant, you should only take advice from people who have accomplished what you're trying to do. You get bad advice from people who have never done the thing you're trying to do. But when you ask David how to defeat a giant, the answer goes something like this.

"Do you know how to use a sling?"

"I do."

"Use that. Do you see his big head that's the size of an 18-wheeler? Hit him right between the eyes. He has no armor there. Then, when he falls, you take his sword and cut his head off. If I were you, I'd go after all the men behind him after you finish that."

Wise men give you a path forward. Wise counselors tell you how to do what you're about to do. What the Bible says in Proverbs 15:22 is very true, *"Plans fail for lack of advisors."*

Are you a pastor getting ready to build a church? How many pastors have you talked to who have successfully built large churches? If you've spoken to none, you're not very bright and you need to change your direction.

Are you anticipating an evangelistic crusade? How many evangelists have you talked to who have successfully done evangelistic crusades?

When I was preparing for an evangelistic crusade in Allentown, Pennsylvania, my father told me, "They probably won't even require it, but make them state the permissible decibel level for your sound on the permit. One way the Devil stops evangelistic crusades is with noise complaints. When people call the police, they will inevitably come. When they do, have someone at the soundboard with a decibel meter. Show them the permit with the stated permissible decibel level and that you're under that. They'll go away. Otherwise, they'll keep coming back and tell you to turn the sound down until your sound is off."

I listened to my father and did what he said in preparation for my crusade. Everything my father said would happen happened. When we said we wanted to know precisely how many decibels we were allowed, they replied, "Oh, it's not going to be a problem. We have concerts in that park all the time. We've had no complaints." But I knew there would be complaints because it's not the noise that bothers people. It's what the noise is about that troubles people's demon spirits.

We set a record for 9-1-1 calls in the city with over 150 calls for noise complaints, even though they've had concerts there frequently with no complaints. The cops came and said, "Hey, we've been getting a lot of noise complaints. We need you to turn the sound down."

But I told them, "No, it says here we're allowed to be at 91 decibels. We're at 89."

The only thing they could say was, "Oh, okay," and they left.

Wise counselors get you ahead of the plan of the Devil. The Devil has no new tricks. People who have been down the road 20 years before you already know how the Devil tries to attack and how to defend against the attacks. I find it baffling who young ministers decide to listen to and who they choose to ignore.

If you're a preacher who values keeping your marriage together and growing your ministry, then whom you follow matters. If you follow a minister with an excellent pulpit ministry and extraordinary meetings, you'll have those things, too. But if he's been in and out of three marriages, has anger issues, and treats people terribly, you'll get the whole impartation. You'll have great meetings, probably treat your wife terribly, and she'll probably leave you. What you see is what you do. Joshua, chapter one says, *"That you may observe to do."* What you observe is what you'll do.

If you follow a minister with an excellent pulpit ministry, but he squanders money, has a cocaine habit, and is always in debt from buying new cars and flashy things—you'll do the same thing. You'll spend too much trying to look like something you're not. Make sure you take note of the whole package. Some people don't listen to anybody, while others listen to stupid people.

…fools despise wisdom and instruction…

— PROVERBS 1:7 (KJV)

Wise people want to learn more, so they listen closely to gain knowledge.

— PROVERBS 18:15 (ERV)

Get all the advice and instruction you can, so you will be wise the rest of your life.

— PROVERBS 19:20

Fools hate when people tell them anything. If the average Christian met Jesus, they would tell Him their testimony—where they live and what's going on in their life. What would you say if you could sit at a table with Jesus? I'll tell you what I'd say: I'd ask what He had to tell me about my life, what I need to change, what I need to do more, and what I need to do less.

Almost every older, notable minister or business person that I've had the chance to meet, I've asked, "If you could go back in time and be my age, what's something that you did that you wouldn't do and what's something that you didn't do that you would do. What's one change you would make?" I don't understand why people always want to tell everybody their story. You could sit at a table with a gold mine and get nothing because you're too busy vomiting the same story you've rehearsed for everyone who comes within ten feet of you. Talk less. Listen more. It's a secret to wisdom.

 What I'm going through will not stop where I'm going.

Don't let it stop you. Don't let it slow you down. Don't let it pause you. Don't let it delay you.

16

LABOR PAINS ARE A SPRINGBOARD TO YOUR DESTINY

God can use an irritation to get you moving. If you've bought a house, what made you go from renting an apartment to buying a home? At some point, you were no longer happy with your landlord, or you got fed up with your neighbors, and eventually, you said, "We need to move." You used to love where you lived. Now, it's getting on your nerves. Pay attention to what irritates you.

Sometimes, you must stand, fight, and run people off the land. Sometimes, running off enemies who take the things God gave you is necessary. But occasionally, God will use an irritation, like labor pains, to tell you it's time to birth the baby. It gets you moving. You've had enough. You've been pushed too far. You can't take it anymore. That's not a time to get discouraged. It's time to decide. It's either time to stand and fight, or you need to realize God, like a pearl produced by the irritation inside the shell, is using this to thrust you toward your destiny. When things feel wrong, rather than get discouraged, maybe that irritation is a signal. God is signaling you to move forward. Pay attention to these irritations.

17
KEEP THE NARRATIVE POSITIVE

If you're in a leadership position, you need to keep the narrative positive while going through a battle. As a leader, you have a duty to make things positive and keep people in a productive frame of mind.

My grandfather, A.E. Shuttlesworth, who was in the ministry for 60 years, often said, "When you don't know what to do, take over."

> Three days later, when David and his men arrived home at their town of Ziklag, they found that the Amalekites had made a raid into the Negev and Ziklag; they had crushed Ziklag and burned it to the ground. They had carried off the women and children and everyone else but without killing anyone.
> When David and his men saw the ruins and realized what had happened to their families, they wept until they could weep no more. David's two wives, Ahinoam from Jezreel and Abigail, the widow of Nabal from Carmel, were among those captured. David was now in great danger

because all his men were very bitter about losing their sons and daughters, and they began to talk of stoning him. But David found strength in the Lord his God.

Then he said to Abiathar the priest, "Bring me the ephod!" So Abiathar brought it. Then David asked the Lord, "Should I chase after this band of raiders? Will I catch them?"

And the Lord told him, "Yes, go after them. You will surely recover everything that was taken from you!"

—1 SAMUEL 30:1-8

 I will pursue, overtake, and recover all.

David and his men had success, just like the Lord said. What was it that stopped David's men from talking about killing him? Imagine that your wife and kids are gone. ISIS took them, and you blame the man in charge. You'd probably say, "Well, I just lost my whole family. I'm going to kill you." That was their thinking. What stopped them from killing David was his plan to move forward.

David told his men, "Listen, we will pursue them. The Lord spoke to me. We're going to catch up to them, and we're going to get everything back. You're going to get all your wives and all your children back." After that, you don't hear any more talk of stoning. What was responsible for the talk of stoning? No course of action. No plan. As a leader, you must give the people under you a plan for moving forward.

If you're a pastor transitioning your church between buildings, people will put up with some temporary discomfort if they know there's a plan forward. Never plan to go backward. Don't go backward. Pursue, overtake, recover all, and give people a plan for moving forward.

Suppose David had communicated his plan from the beginning and said, "Our wives and kids aren't here. Everybody saddle up. We'll get them back right now." There wouldn't have been any time to sit around talking about killing the leader. But if you go silent or take an eight-month sabbatical, there's no telling what you'll return to.

Leaders must show the path forward without having to make it up. You're commanded to be fruitful, increase, and multiply. You receive that from God and show people where you're headed.

Whenever the Devil throws something at you to make you take a step backward, find a plan from God to make it backfire. Turn negativity into a significant positive. That's the fun of being a leader. When you get hit with challenges, see it like David. All things are scripturally mandated to work together for your good. Since you love God and are called according to His purpose, then pray, "Father, show me how to flip this situation around." Communicate forward movement to your people.

When COVID hit and the stock market crashed, some ministries preemptively laid off a third of their staff. I'm sure the people who worked for our ministry were nervous. So I called them all in and said, "So that you know, nobody is going to lose their job or have their salary reduced during this health thing." How was I supposed to guarantee that? Do it anyway. It's your job as a leader. If you stay quiet, it gives room for Absaloms to rise up and start creating their own narrative.

Keep vocal leadership in front of your people, business, or ministry. Otherwise, people start coming up with their own insane ideas of what's happening and more insane ideas of how to deal with it. Most problems in life can be solved by one conversation—not all, but most. If you get hit by a bus, you need urgent medical care; a conversation can't solve that. But most problems, especially leadership problems, can be solved with one conversation.

It's easy to hate someone who remains distant and doesn't communicate. Then, when you meet them, you realize they're actually not that bad. There are very few people who you won't like after meeting them. Humans build a person up in their heads based on what people tell them, but it's a different story when you meet them.

All this sabbatical stuff is a mess. I would never do it. You can't take six months off as a leader. You can't take three months off as a leader. I don't know if you could take three weeks off as a leader—that would be pushing it.

Keep the narrative positive—without lying. You should have a forward direction, regardless of what challenges you face.

18

ONLY FIGHT YOUR ENEMY

Don't allow your fight to affect your family. As a leader, you need to learn to switch gears when you are at home. I had to learn this. It's not helpful for your marriage to talk to your wife or husband in the same tone of voice you use to cast out demons. It doesn't make for the most positive marriage.

When you're in fight mode or going through a battle in life, switch gears when you come home. Spend peaceful time with your wife and children. There must come a time when you're done fighting for the day. Turn your phone off, or don't take texts or calls from certain people for the rest of the day. Pick it up tomorrow. You can't stay in fight mode 24 hours a day.

What good is it to win your battle but lose your family? If you win a 2-year legal battle, but it strains your marriage because you always fought with your spouse, that demonstrates immaturity. Learn only to fight your enemy. Love your wife and children. God will help you do these things, but most people won't make the effort. They're often a super great husband and father, but they suck at fighting. They're just a pushover. Or they're fighters who never lose a battle, but their marriage is on the rocks—or over—and their children hate them because they're constantly in fight mode.

You must learn to switch gears. Fight when it's time to fight, and only fight your enemies. When it's not time to fight anymore, quit fighting.

19

DON'T BE NEGATIVE

In the previous point, I mentioned not allowing the fight to affect your relationship with your family. It's also important not to let your fight affect you personally; sometimes, it does without you realizing it.

During COVID, many pastors kept their churches open while under a barrage of attacks for 18 months. In the United States, that pressure is no longer present. The Department of Health is not threatening to close churches. Governors aren't saying they're going to act against your church. That's ended. But what many pastors went through over those 18 months has made them very negative.

When Satan attacks, he's not just looking to win that battle; he's looking to steal, kill, and destroy. If you win the battle but lose your joy, you're no longer enjoyable to be around. Don't become a negative person. Keep your joy amid the fight and keep your joy after the fight.

Some people are so negative after all their battles that they can't even receive victory anymore. Don't allow your battle to turn you into a negative person. Stay positive. You should be fun to be around, and you should make people laugh.

> May you be strengthened with all power, according to his glorious might, for all endurance and patience with joy.

— COLOSSIANS 1:11 (RSV)

2 0

BUFFERS

This is a practical way to stay in victory. It may be the most useful of all the keys in this book.

Always think like this: If I were the Devil, how would I attack my ministry? If I were the Devil, how would I attack my business? How would I attack my home?

Demons can't just come and load your church into a demon U-Haul and carry it off. Satan has to use people. *"The heavens are the Lord's, But the earth He has given to the children of men"* (Psalms 115:16). Satan uses people. People don't buy drugs from demons. There are demonized people, like Sanballat and Tobiah in the book of Nehemiah, who seek to take you down.

Ask yourself, "If I was the Devil, in what ways would I attack my business or ministry?" The number one way to do so in America and most countries is through finances. Want to know how I put a buffer between me and the Devil to keep him from doing what he wants to do? I told Patrick, our ministry CFO, to make sure our record keeping is such that if an IRS agent walked in and said, "You have one week to submit your financial forms because we suspect you've committed fraud." His response should be, "Oh, no, I don't need a week. Here are all our records, there's not one shady thing going on."

Finances are the primary way an enemy will come after your ministry and most businesses. Make sure everything is clean financially. Know the laws and go above and beyond what the law requires—no gray areas.

When you're small, people don't care what you're doing, but everyone cares if you get to the Elon Musk level, or even half the Elon Musk level, or 15 percent of where Elon Musk is. They're going to use every law they can against you.

In the book of Daniel, before they made the law that he couldn't pray, the Bible says they searched every way to find a violation so they could arrest him. I don't mean to imply that you need to be open with your finances as a ministry or business. You don't have to do that—It's nobody's business. But you should have everything in perfect order. When I'm done preaching, I don't go anywhere near where the offering is counted. I don't take a fist full of hundreds to take people out to lunch. I don't use my ministry credit card to buy personal meals or personal gas.

We conduct an independent audit every year through an external accounting firm. The IRS is just going to waste money auditing me. I've already been audited in the past. If the IRS wants to do it again, they can be my guest.

We don't pay people under the table. If I were the Devil, I would target construction companies known for paying under the table. I'd send somebody in and have them record that they were paid under the table and didn't have any documentation for the work, and I'd turn them in.

If I were the Devil, I'd send somebody to shoot up my church. That's why we have buffers, so that can never happen. You'd never get the weapon out of its holster or wherever you hid it. We don't allow backpacks in the sanctuary.

I've visited many churches, and I've quickly realized they've never given one minute of thought to finances or the safety of people. That's why we have catchers when you lay hands on people. Why must you catch them if it's of the Holy Spirit? Because some people come into prayer lines to fall over and claim they were injured so they can sue the church—that's why.

If I were the Devil, I'd send a lady to make sexual harassment claims against me and my ministry. That's why my life is set up so no one can ever say they were in a room with me alone or without video cameras.

Let me give you two important safety buffers for ministry—they also apply to most businesses.

1. Carefully consider who counts and handles your money.

I was preaching at a church, and the Holy Spirit spoke to the pastor for whom I was preaching. He said, "I think the lady who counts our offerings is stealing the money."

I asked, "Who counts it with her?"

"Oh, she counts it by herself."

Well, that's a problematic and sloppy system. There should be three to nine people in charge of counting the offering. They should be on rotations where two or three count the offering together. It's tough to get nine people to conspire to steal money. If you're constantly mixing who's counting, one person can't partner with another. Some churches have the same two people count the offering every Sunday—not intelligent.

The pastor said, "I think the lady steals our money. She counts it. She makes the deposit on Monday. But I don't know what to do."

The Lord gave me a plan. I suggested he tell her he will have someone else count the money and make the deposit to free her up for other stuff he's getting ready to add to the church. Tell her someone on staff will handle the deposit and that she doesn't need to do menial work like that. Make it seem like a promotion. If she responds with gratitude, you'll know she wasn't stealing. If she gets angry over giving her one less thing to do, you'll know she's a thief.

She got angry when he nicely told her she didn't have to count the offerings anymore. He had taken a source of income away from her. This leads me to buffer number two.

2. Protect what's been entrusted to you.

If you always think the best of everyone, you will be taken. One thing you'll notice about the Devil is that he doesn't like attacking things that are well-protected. He strikes soft targets. For instance, churches that get shot up usually don't have any security.

Think how often you walk past a kiosk or a store in the mall, and the salesperson is just sitting there talking on their phone. They're supposed to be selling. That's what they're getting paid to do. When you walk past some kiosks, the people are like mosquitoes; they won't leave you alone. Then, you have other people sitting there and texting without looking up.

I bring this up because if you own something, you had better monitor it. When I walk by those kiosks or stores, I think about how somebody invested their life in that business. They had to get a loan and borrow against the value of their home to make a go of this business and then put some unproven 24-year-old in charge who didn't care about them or their family. The owner obviously never comes by and checks on their own business.

Put buffers in place and monitor what's going on.

 People change.

Judas wasn't demon-possessed when Jesus made him a disciple. A demon entered Judas at the tail end of his three-and-a-half years with Jesus. You can hire somebody who's an honest person—they were great when you hired them. But people can get wrapped up in things like pornography, drugs, and alcohol, and it changes them.

I could hire somebody who's honest and would never steal money. But if they get hooked on cocaine or heroin, and I don't know anything about it, they'll start stealing money. You have to keep an eye on people.

I've told our ministry leadership to watch people who miss prayer every afternoon. There are certain behaviors people exhibit when they get into sin. They avoid the anointing.

You must create buffers. Think, 'How would I attack my life, business, and ministry if I were the Devil?'

I've been to churches with a security program as good as our church, but I've never been to one better. You couldn't have better. Why would Jesus entrust His sheep to a shepherd who makes no provision to deal with wolves? Jesus is the head of the Church. He doesn't want His sheep to be slaughtered. He wants them protected.

Guard what the Lord has given you. Create buffers.

21

USE THE LAW OF
ENCOURAGEMENT

The generous will prosper; those who refresh others will themselves be refreshed.

— PROVERBS 11:25

When going through a battle, it's easy to get discouraged. How do you make sure you never become discouraged? When you need something, sow for it. If you want friends, show yourself to be friendly and sow the seed of friendship. If you need money, sow money. If you're going through a discouraging time, encourage and refresh others. Proverbs 11:25 says, *"Those who refresh others will themselves be refreshed."*

It's impossible to lack what you sow. Don't go around telling people, "I've been discouraged lately." You're letting people know you don't encourage anyone.

Whatever you need, sow for it. When you're battling discouragement, that's the time to refresh and encourage as many people as you can because you're the one who will reap the benefit.

22

ADOPT AN AGGRESSIVE MINDSET

Any consequences you face should be due to your aggressive mindset.

During the COVID pandemic, some pastors defied unconstitutional orders under threat of arrest and losing their church—although very few did. The *authorities* never showed up to make good on their threats. The few pastors who were arrested have booming churches now—their finances are booming, too.

If you face consequences for your actions, it should be for your aggressive actions. That's the principle of David and Goliath. You're going to face consequences either way. Do you want the consequences to be for failing to fight Goliath? Would you rather have the Philistines make you their slaves or decide as David did, "If I'm going to die, I'll die, but I'm not dying as a slave? I'm going to die as somebody who confronted the one who wanted to enslave me."

Do it with wisdom, not recklessly. But decide that if you fail, it will be because you went too far forward, not because you were afraid to move forward. Please get this in your spirit.

It's often more dangerous to be safe. As we learn from David and Goliath, it's safest on the battlefield. The place of true safety is the place of confronting your adversary.

In Arizona, I got a book on tape about Lake Powell. It was named after a man named J.W. Powell, who only had one arm. In his day, no one had ever mapped the Grand Canyon because the terrain was too rugged. It was the last unmapped area of the United States. The Green River that turns into the Colorado River runs through there. Powell put ten guys and four canoes in the Colorado River. They did not know if a Niagara Falls-type situation was ahead of them. They decided to go for it.

The rapids grew worse each day. Eventually, men began to turn back. Three of the remaining nine men decided it would be suicide to continue down the river in the canoes. The rapids kept getting worse each day, and they barely survived thus far. The three who quit decided to hike up the Grand Canyon and find the nearest Mormon village. The other six men decided to go the rest of the way.

The six who didn't quit went through the intense rapids and made it out uninjured, just sunburned with their rotten food. The three who played it safe made it out of the Grand Canyon and were killed by Native Americans. A Native American woman had been raped, and it was assumed the three strangers did it, so the Native Americans killed them in retaliation.

Never sell off your destiny for the illusion of short-term comfort and safety.

Here's another example of how it pays to be aggressive. There's a base camp for people who want to quit halfway up Mount Everest. The quitters are the happiest people you'll ever see when they quit. But when everybody comes back down from the summit and meets them again, they look like they're contemplating suicide. They paid good money to climb Mount Everest, but they were going home to tell everybody they only went halfway up because the air was really thin, and their chest was hurting. They had the chance of a lifetime to climb Mount Everest, and they blew it.

In Numbers, chapters thirteen and fourteen, the ten spies who thought they were playing it safe died, and the two who decided the Lord was with them—"we should go at once and take the land and possess it from Jordan to the sea"—didn't die. You're safest when moving forward.

No one ever flat-out says, "I quit." People devise many creative ways to say, "I'm a coward." Nobody ever actually says, "I'm a coward. I quit." Initially, quitting feels safe, but moving forward is safest because there is no anointing for retreating. You'll never read in the Bible where the Spirit of the Lord came upon David, and he ran away, or the Spirit of the Lord came upon the Israelites, and they hid from the people of Jericho.

If you don't plan to move forward, you subconsciously plan to stay at the same level. That's dangerous. When you quit moving forward, you start losing people. The excitement leaves. There's no thrill in the ministry anymore. The thrill is in taking new ground. The thrill is in growing your business, not maintaining your business. God is not interested in maintaining the status quo.

There are two *M* words: one that God is not interested in and another that God is very interested in. He's not interested in *maintaining*; He's interested in *multiplying*. God is never in anything that's against your multiplication.

I make plans to advance with force so I can be safe. Sitting still leads to death. God is not interested in maintaining what you have, but in multiplying what you have. You will multiply all this year, in Jesus' name.

Wherever you've been stopped, you will advance past that point. What you're going through will not stop you from where you're going any more than the storm kept Jesus from going over to the other side.

God can use negative things from your past and turn them into something positive, whereby you no longer have fear.

I mandate you to move forward forcefully for the rest of this year. Get a plan from God and attack.

2 3

SURROUND YOURSELF WITH LIKE-MINDS

During COVID, I decided that if I were going to make a mistake, it would be for defying the mandate by preaching and maybe getting arrested. It's not going to be the mistake of allowing my ministry—which I've worked and built for over 19 years—to be choked out because I chose the supposed "safe" thing.

If I had shut down, all the phone calls would have gone away. All the death threats would have stopped. Local news people would no longer corner me by a dumpster to ask me why I chose to put the whole city at risk. That would have all gone away if I had just done what my enemy told me.

If you're going to make a mistake, make it by being too aggressive, and you'll discover that it's actually hard to make a mistake that way. If we make a mistake, it will result from being too aggressive and defying something wrong, not tip-toeing because it's considered wise or virtuous.

As little kids in Sunday School, they used to tell us that when you picture the armor of God—the helmet, the breastplate of righteousness, the shield of faith, the sword of the spirit, the whole armor—all the armor is in the front. There's no armor on the back because there's no protection from God for retreating. As soon as you turn your back, you have no protection.

Make your mistakes by being aggressive. What the Devil means for bad is turned to good through your righteous aggression.

When Rodney Howard-Browne got arrested during COVID, everybody in the ministry world said he was making a mistake. Sean Hannity, who's supposed to be conservative, called him a grandstanding Florida pastor who wants his name in the papers. But when all the dust settled, his church tripled in size. All the people who, by "wisdom," shut down—if they even have a ministry left—are down to 20 percent of what they were before. Always think long-term. Put up with temporary pain to advance. As you hold to the principles of the Bible and remain obedient to the things God's called you to do as a believer, not everyone will approve.

If a news feature about you aired and painted you as the worst person in the community for some reason, most people would probably believe it. But there will be one or two percent of people like you who will take a stand. If those one or two percent of people come to your church or your business, that equals a lot of people. It's a lot of free advertising.

Make your mistakes by being aggressive. Don't be a coward. If you could turn back time two and a half years, people would still shut down their churches and businesses. Knowing what we know now, many people who closed down would decide to stay open. They now realize it was unconstitutional.

There's a restaurant in Pittsburgh that refused to shut down or to make people wear masks. Now, they're packed. They just expanded.

I eat there. If their food goes downhill, I'll still eat there to support the stand they made.

If you seek to make your mistakes being aggressive, you need a board of directors or leadership with the same mindset. I could never have stayed open if I carried my ministry credentials with the Assemblies of God or the Church of God. They threatened to pull the credentials of any minister who kept their ministries open. How can two walk together unless they agree? If you're going to be aggressive, surround yourself with aggressive people.

24
KEEP YOUR FIGHTING SPIRIT

There's a risk of becoming like King David, who, in the season when kings went to war, stayed home. The question is: why did David decide to stay home?

He probably figured, "I've been fighting since I was 17. From the day I killed Goliath, I've had to fight the men behind him. Then King Saul turned on me. I had to fight his guys. I'm going to sit this one out."

That's an easy conclusion because the fights don't stop—you'll face much bigger opponents. The fight doesn't stop until Jesus gives you a crown and says, "Well done, my good and faithful servant." When we go to Heaven and have the marriage supper of the lamb, that's your victory party. Until then, it's not time to celebrate.

My dad told me something at the beginning of COVID. He said, once a runner, always a runner. He meant that if you back down, you'll always back down.

I've heard prominent pastors in South Africa talk about how the government is intruding. The government may require vaccine passports to go to church in South Africa. The South African pastors claim they will not go along with this government intrusion. But they will because many have done everything they were told to do over the last three years. It's hard to believe they're not going to listen when they have a mask over their faces while claiming they won't listen to what the government tells them to do. They already did.

Once you retreat, you'll keep retreating. When Elijah backed down in 1 Kings chapter nineteen, God told him to go and anoint Elisha in his stead. When you bow out of the fight, you head toward eternity.

The average person dies within seven years of retirement. Man wasn't created for rest. Man was created for work. You have to rest, but in business, you should always have something fresh that you're doing for the Lord. As soon as you become like David and decide you've had enough of this and stay behind, problems set in.

Inaction makes room for sin. If David had been out fighting, he wouldn't have had time to be up on his roof, looking at who was taking baths. There's no time to sin when you stay busy with your assignment. Don't allow yourself to become tired.

 I'm going to do this until it's done.

When your flesh feels tired, speak the opposite out of your mouth. "You think I'm tired? I'm just getting warmed up." Start talking like that. Your body will come in line with what you speak. Never let "I'm tired" come out of your mouth.

Subconsciously, if you're not vigilant, you'll find yourself inclined to take it easy during the crucial years of 40, 45, 50, 55, or 60—in the season when kings go to war.

Have you stopped fighting? Are you still expanding? Don't lose your fighting spirit. In the season when kings go to war, you should go to war.

When was the last time your business hired a new employee? We started 2022 with 14. I was hoping to stay at 14, to be honest. However, by the time this book is released, we'll have 53 full-time employees. Nobody is here by faith or volunteering.

 Expand, increase, multiply.

Therefore, you must monitor whether you've quit fighting. No one ever says, "You know what, I've given up on life. Oh, I quit three years ago. I don't try anymore." No one says that. You gauge it by the fruit you're producing.

When was the last time you acquired a new property? When was the last time you hired a new employee? What's the last big move you've made?

Who you hang around determines where you go in life. I'm hanging around people who build new buildings like they're tree houses, and that grace is rubbing off on this ministry.

Keep fighting. Keep going forward. Don't quit.

When you stop taking new ground, you quit without knowing it. That's one reason why I take an extended vacation. I rest hard and then hit it hard. That's what Jesus did—withdraw to the wilderness and come back teaching, preaching, and laying hands on people.

In the Scripture that I started with, God's solution for Elijah feeling so discouraged was for him to sleep. Then, God had an angel make pancakes and give him a drink. When he finished eating them, He had the angel make him more pancakes.

Don't lose your fighting spirit. Don't allow yourself to get tired and beaten up. Get a different face, stand up straight, and go forward. If people don't know you, they shouldn't be able to tell you've been through anything.

> When David saw them whispering, he realized what had happened. "Is the child dead?" he asked.
> "Yes," they replied, "he is dead."
> Then David got up from the ground, washed himself, put on lotions, and changed his clothes. He went to the Tabernacle and worshiped the Lord. After that, he returned to the palace and was served food and ate.
> His advisers were amazed. "We don't understand you," they told him. "While the child was still living, you wept and refused to eat. But now that the child is dead, you have stopped your mourning and are eating again."
> David replied, "I fasted and wept while the child was alive, for I said, 'Perhaps the Lord will be gracious to me and let the child live.' But why should I fast when he is dead? Can I bring him back again? I will go to him one day, but he cannot return to me."
>
> — 2 SAMUEL 12:19-23

Once the crisis ended, David dressed, put on cologne, and said, "I'm done with this thing." Most people do the opposite, but David decided it was pointless to fast when his son was dead. He knew he couldn't bring the child back. He said. "I'll go [to heaven and see him] one day, but he cannot return to me." If you've lost a child and you're wondering where the child is, this is a good scripture for you. *"I can't bring him back to me, but I will go to him one day"* (2 Samuel 12:23).

When you go through a tragedy, you must decide, "I'm done with that. I did what I could. I did the best I could. I'm not going to let it affect me. I can't change what happened, but I can ensure it doesn't affect me going forward." Don't drag it with you and allow it to affect your countenance.

Losing a loved one, whether it's a spouse, parent, or anyone close to you, is an incredibly challenging experience. We had a man in our church not too long ago who went through the heart-wrenching loss of his child. His grief was so overwhelming that he reached the point of contemplating taking his own life. I'm not suggesting you should pretend or be insincere, but handling it as David did is essential. The first place David went after he bathed and got changed was to the Tabernacle. Get your grief and despair under the blood. There's an anointing that binds up the broken-hearted. When tragedy strikes, seek that anointing.

Deal with things from your past. One way you can tell it's dealt with is when someone can bring up the topic, and it doesn't devastate you.

The Bible says there is a time to mourn with those who mourn. People don't need some trite statement from you. Just hug them. When people write to me about something horrific that happened, and somebody in their family died, I'll just put the emoji heart, the emoji praying hands, and write, "I love you."

I heard a good saying: "Grief is love with no place to go." You have all this love in your heart for somebody, and now there's nowhere to put it. But there comes a time when you must put that thing to bed like David did.

John 10:10 says, *"The thief comes to steal, kill, and destroy,"* but it doesn't have to happen. If you've lost somebody, as King David did, there comes a time when you have to put it to bed. You have to get a hold on it so it doesn't have a hold on you. Not that you forget or refuse to talk about it, because that's weird, too.

You can get weird in two ways when it comes to a tragedy. You can become obsessed with it to the point where it gets weird, but you can also get weird by pretending it didn't happen.

There's nothing wrong with mourning for a period—a defined period. But after a season, you must let it go and move on; don't carry it forward. Because the thief that comes to steal and kill, if you're not careful, that death will destroy other things.

Too often, after somebody has lost someone close to them, they become a different person. They haven't been to work in five months. They're three mortgage payments behind. What's happening? Destruction. Decide as David did. You might not change that thing, but you can decide not to drag it forward into your future.

Nobody is a better example than pastor Rodney Howard-Browne. What do you do when your 18-year-old daughter passes away on Christmas morning? What do you do after there's a death, a tragic and unexpected loss? You may not have been able to stop the second part of Satan's plan, but make sure you stop the third part.

Death is not of God. Even if you live 120 years, God never created people to die. You can thank Satan for that—he brought death through sin.

I'm not going to allow it to affect my income. I'm not going to take three months off work. You have to be careful because there is a feeling that can rise in you when you lose somebody close to you, causing you to think you'll cancel a few things and take a week to feel better. Let me tell you, on day eight, you're not going to feel any more like doing anything than you did on day one. I suggest that, as much as possible, you stay in the flow of what you're doing and then maybe take a break down the line.

Only the Holy Ghost can bind up a broken heart. Jesus said, *"The spirit of the Lord is upon me, for he has anointed me to bind up the broken-hearted."* (Isaiah 61:1).

> Meanwhile, Joab was fighting against Rabbah, the capital of Ammon, and he captured the royal fortifications. Joab sent messengers to tell David, "I have fought against Rabbah and captured its water supply. Now bring the rest of the army and capture the city. Otherwise, I will capture it and get credit for the victory."
> So David gathered the rest of the army and went to Rabbah, and he fought against it and captured it. David removed the crown from the king's head, and it was placed on his own head. The crown was made of gold and set with gems, and it weighed seventy-five pounds.
>
> — 2 SAMUEL 12:26-30

What do you do after a setback? Go forward. Instead of letting the Devil destroy something of yours, destroy something of the Devil's. Don't let the Devil destroy your peace, sanity, or business. Instead, go destroy something of his.

When you win souls, you're destroying something of the Devil's. You're taking something out of his kingdom. You're destroying his chains. You're destroying his prison. *"For this reason, the Son of God was made manifest that He might destroy the work of the Devil"* (1 John 3:8).

The goal of Christianity is not to sit back and try not to be destroyed. People who rob people don't get robbed while they're robbing. You don't get attacked when you're on the attack because you're too busy attacking. Attackers don't get attacked. Sitters get attacked.

Stop sitting in your living room. Do something that focuses your mind on an objective. That's what David did after he had to bury his son. One paragraph later, he goes out and captures a city.

If the Devil destroyed something in your life through sickness and disease, destroy his realm of sickness and disease by healing the sick. Do what David did—decide. You can't change what happened, but you can change the future.

 Satan, you may have stolen, you may have killed, but you will not destroy!

If you're going to experience peace, the only real peace comes from knowing Jesus Christ. It's what saved David. Through his covenant with God, he knew he would see his loved one again. The Bible says we don't mourn like those who have no hope. But to mourn like those who have hope, you must be in covenant with God.

When Christ comes into your heart, He heals your soul. If you've never received Jesus Christ, or you've allowed a tragedy to put distance between you and your relationship with God, Satan will use that to destroy you. More than your business shutting down or anything else, he'd want to use tragedy to create distance between you and God. Be like the prodigal son and return to Him today, and you'll find Him waiting with open arms.

AFTERWORD

> When Ahab got home, he told Jezebel everything Elijah had
> done, including the way he had killed all the prophets of
> Baal. So Jezebel sent this message to Elijah: "May the gods
> strike me and even kill me if by this time tomorrow I have
> not killed you just as you killed them."
>
> — 1 KINGS 19:1-2

Now, Elijah had just then called fire down from heaven. He had just
set his nation free from demonic bondage. What was his reward? Directly after, one of the heads of his government said, "May the gods
strike me dead if by this time tomorrow I haven't killed Elijah," and
word got back to him.

I didn't understand this principle for a long time. I thought everyone
who got in trouble with the government, attracted negative attention, or was portrayed negatively on the five o'clock news brought it
on themselves. I used to think it was obvious: if you have a good
heart and good intentions, people will love you. I must have missed

the part of the Bible where Jesus said, *"I have done many good works. For which one are you going to stone me?"* To which they replied, *"We're stoning you not for any good work, but for blasphemy! You, a mere man, claim to be God"* (John 10:32-33).

One thing you need to know in life, ministry, and business is that Elijah did nothing wrong. He did something right. Jesus did nothing wrong. If He did, we're all going to Hell if He sinned, but He never sinned.

Life has battles.

> Elijah was afraid and fled for his life. He went to Beersheba, a town in Judah, and he left his servant there. Then he went on alone into the wilderness, traveling all day. He sat down under a solitary broom tree and prayed that he might die. "I have had enough, Lord," he said. "Take my life, for I am no better than my ancestors who have already died."
>
> — 1 KINGS 19:3-4

I've had to use the keys covered in this book several times. I've engaged in the art of spiritual warfare recently.

A nearby church got upset over how many people we had come to our Easter service. They took photographs of the service and reported how many people were present, turned me into the city, and demanded our church be shut down. I dealt with that for about six weeks and received a favorable outcome. I was teaching on spiritual warfare amid the battle because it was on my heart. That situation was not my first rodeo, nor will it be my last.

When you do what God wants, the Devil doesn't just say, "You know what? Look at the good heart this person has. Look at him winning souls. You know what, demons, let's just leave him alone." No. What do you see with Elijah? What do you see with the apostle Paul? Paul's thorn in the flesh.

> This boasting will do no good, but I must go on. I will reluctantly tell about visions and revelations from the Lord. I was caught up to the third heaven fourteen years ago. Whether I was in my body or out of my body, I don't know—only God knows. Yes, only God knows whether I was in my body or outside my body. But I do know that I was caught up to paradise and heard things so astounding that they cannot be expressed in words, things no human is allowed to tell.
>
> That experience is worth boasting about, but I'm not going to do it. I will boast only about my weaknesses. If I wanted to boast, I would be no fool in doing so, because I would be telling the truth. But I won't do it, because I don't want anyone to give me credit beyond what they can see in my life or hear in my message, even though I have received such wonderful revelations from God. So to keep me from becoming proud, I was given a thorn in my flesh, a messenger from Satan to torment me and keep me from becoming proud.
>
> — 2 CORINTHIANS 12:1-7

This boasting will do no good, but I must go on. Paul's thorn in the flesh was a messenger from Satan, not cancer. You're allowing the Devil to twist scripture to get you to accept sickness and disease if you believe Paul's thorn was a physical ailment of any kind.

So to keep me from becoming proud, I was given a thorn in
my flesh, a messenger from Satan to torment me and keep
me from becoming proud.

Three different times I begged the Lord to take it away. Each
time he said, "My grace is all you need. My power works
best in weakness." So now I am glad to boast about my
weaknesses, so that the power of Christ can work through
me. That's why I take pleasure in my weaknesses, and in
the insults, hardships, persecutions, and troubles that I
suffer for Christ. For when I am weak, then I am strong.

— 2 CORINTHIANS 12:7-10

Paul's thorn in the flesh was government opposition and satanic
opposition to his advancement.

In Acts chapter 16, a little servant girl who was demon-possessed
kept coming behind him and yelling. He told the demon inside of
her to shut up and come out of her, and her two masters had him
arrested and thrown in prison. Paul was bouncing in and out of jail
more than Suge Knight.

That's what his thorn was. What did Paul do wrong? He didn't do
anything wrong. What did Elijah do wrong? He didn't do anything
wrong. What did Jesus do wrong? He did nothing wrong.

Bible school teaches you to go out and win the world and will have
you believe you will be incredibly blessed for doing so. Many people
are blessed; many within Jesus' ministry were blessed. But there are
people under the control of the Devil, and when they see you setting
people free and building the Kingdom of God, they get a fire in them
from Hell to shut your business, church, or evangelistic ministry
down.

Maybe you thought that because you became a Christian and went into the ministry, everything would go smoothly as long as you did what was right. When things don't go smoothly, don't do what Elijah did and back off. A paragraph later, Elijah is contemplating suicide.

When you face a battle, stand up and fight. That's the only way forward. Resist the Devil, and he'll flee from you. *"Watch ye, stand fast in the faith, quit you like men, be strong"* (1 Corinthians 16:13). Stand and fight!

The way forward is to stand against your opposition.

"By this time tomorrow, may the gods kill me if you're not dead." Jezebel wasn't threatening him with a lawsuit. Jezebel was threatening to kill him.

Whatever you may go through in the Western world is far less than what our Christian brothers and sisters in Pakistan go through. So, fight. Even if you're in Pakistan, fight.

During COVID, many churches shut down because they were afraid of the disease. Many shut down because they got a barrage of comments and negative reviews. Even if I was thinking of making a move for safety's sake, if my enemy wants me to do something, I won't do it. Never let your course of action be dictated to you by your enemy.

You need to know that life is a fight. It's a sign that you're on the right path. The Devil is a big talker and a poor fighter.

"By this time tomorrow, may the gods kill me if you're not dead." Did Jezebel kill Elijah? No. Did she die instead? Yes.

When you're in covenant with the Lord, the Devil can't take you out. He can only threaten you and discourage you into quitting. If you are not in a covenant relationship with God, you can change that situation immediately. No decision you make will impact your life and eternity more than this. Pray this prayer aloud and receive God's forgiveness and salvation:

Heavenly Father, I believe You raised Jesus from the dead. I give You my life today and confess that Jesus is my Lord and Savior. I turn my back on sin and receive Your forgiveness. I want to live for You. In Jesus' name, amen.

If you prayed that prayer, tell me about your decision so we can send you some materials to help you start your new life. Go to this link: revivaltoday.com/just-got-saved.

The Revival Today staff is available to pray with you. Call 412-787-2578 to speak and pray with a real person who cares about you.

Let me be the first to congratulate you on making this important decision that will benefit you, your children, and generations to come. Welcome to your new family, the family of God!

AUTHOR PHOTO

"My generation shall be saved!"

— JONATHAN SHUTTLESWORTH

ABOUT THE AUTHOR

Evangelist and Pastor, Jonathan Shuttlesworth, is the founder of Revival Today and Pastor of Revival Today Church, ministries dedicated to reaching lost and hurting people with The Gospel of Jesus Christ.

In fulfilling his calling, Jonathan Shuttlesworth has conducted meetings and open-air crusades throughout North America, India, the Caribbean, and Central and South Africa.

Revival Today Church was launched in 2022 as a soul-winning, Holy Spirit-honoring church that is unapologetic about believing the Bible to bless families and nations.

Each day thousands of lives are impacted globally through Revival Today Broadcasting and Revival Today Church, located in Pittsburgh, Pennsylvania.

While methods may change, Revival Today's heartbeat remains for the lost, providing biblical teaching on faith, healing, prosperity, freedom from sin, and living a victorious life.

If you need help or would like to partner with Revival Today to see this generation and nation transformed through The Gospel, follow these links…

www.RevivalToday.com
www.RevivalTodayChurch.com

Get access to our 24/7 network Revival Today Global Broadcast.
Download the Revival Today app in your Apple App Store or Google
Play Store. Watch live on Apple TV, Roku, Amazon Fire TV, and
Android TV.

Call: 412-787-2578

facebook.com/revivaltoday
x.com/jdshuttlesworth
instagram.com/jdshuttlesworth
youtube.com/@jonathanshuttlesworth

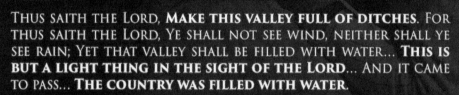

Printed in the USA
CPSIA information can be obtained
at www.ICGtesting.com
LVHW062005170424
777707LV00014B/268